GRACE BASED parenting

VIDEO SERIES

Creating an Atmosphere of Grace

Dr. Tim Kimmel

Name _____

Family Matters
Scottsdale, Arizona 85267
1.800.467.4596
FamilyMatters.net

This workbook is to be used in conjunction with the *Grace Based Parenting Video Series: Creating an Atmosphere of Grace* and is not meant to be a stand alone piece.

Requests for information should be addressed to:

building grace-based relationships

Family Matters®
P.O. Box 14382
Scottsdale, AZ 85267-4382
FamilyMatters.net
800.467.4596

Published by Family Matters®

Cover and interior design by Union Digital (www.uniondigitalmedia.com)

Printed in the United States of America

V7.1.14

Contents

GRACE BASED
parenting
VIDEO SERIES

About Your Speaker

Dr. Tim Kimmel has been a champion of families all of his professional life. As Executive Director of Family Matters, Tim helps families face the future with confidence by teaching them how to bring the best out of each other today. Tim's blue-collar heart and street-level attitude about life allow him to connect to audiences where they live. At the same time, his academic résumé gives him a studied approach to matters of the heart and family.

Dr. Kimmel speaks throughout North America conducting conferences on parenting, grandparenting and marriage. He is a frequent guest on radio and television and has authored many books including *Little House on the Freeway*, *Grace Based Parenting* and *Raising Kids for True Greatness*.

Tim received his doctorate from Western Seminary, his master's degree from Dallas Theological Seminary and his bachelor's degree from Bryan College. Tim does not consider himself an expert, but rather a veteran when it comes to the dynamics of family. His greatest earthly joy comes from his marriage to his high school sweetheart, Darcy, their four children (Karis, Cody, Shiloh and Colt), their children's spouses, and an ever-expanding group of grandchildren.

Welcome!

Thanks for caring enough to take time out of your busy schedules to learn how to be a grace based parent.

Obviously, no parent is guaranteed that as a result of their best efforts, their children will turn out the way they'd like. But we do know that we can increase that likelihood if we understand the "big picture" of our role in their lives and follow some specific principles of effective parenting. Your love for your children has motivated you to make this investment of time and energy to learn those roles and principles. That's why I'm glad you are participating in this study.

You are highly valued. Not only are you important to me, but your family is as well. It is my hope and prayer that God will be free to tug at your heart as you go through this study so that you can enjoy a clear sense of His direction and leadership as you create an atmosphere of grace in your home.

A Special Word to Single Parents and Couples With Blended Families

It is our hope that through this study you might gain some practical insights for your unique family situation. Since this material is taken from the timeless and well-proven truth of the Scriptures, these principles can be adapted to all kinds of family dynamics.

Some of you come with extra needs and circumstances that are outside of your control. One of the best ways you can get the most out of this study is to have realistic expectations of yourself and others. If you are from a blended family, you might want to concentrate your applications on the children you influence the most. If you are a single parent, we encourage you to take into account your energy and resources as you establish your goals.

Regardless of the configuration of your family, God can use you to implant His grace into your children's hearts and aim them at a future of true greatness.
God bless you!

Because Every Family Matters,

Tim Kimmel

GRACE BASED parenting

VIDEO SERIES

Creating an Atmosphere of Grace

Session 1

The Big Picture of Grace Based Parenting

Introduction

God left behind a job description for parents that want to raise

_____ _____.

    A. God wants us to raise kids who love Him, live for Him, and make an

        _____ in their world.

> He answered: "'Love the Lord your God with all your heart and with all
> your soul and with all your strength and with all your mind'; and, 'Love
> your neighbor as yourself.'" Luke 10:27

    B. God has given us the perfect vehicle to make this happen – His

        _____!

> Each one should use whatever gift he has received to serve others,
> faithfully administering God's grace in its various forms. 1 Peter 4:10

**I. Understanding the role of grace in a family frees parents up to raise kids
who make an extraordinary _____ with their lives.**

    A. Grace is not so much what we do, but _____ we do
what we do.

> Instead, speaking the truth in love, we will in all things grow up into Him
> who is the Head, that is, Christ. Ephesians 4:15

B. Grace-based parenting is simply treating your children the way God treats His!

> *For the law was given through Moses; **grace and truth** came through Jesus Christ.* John 1:17, emphasis added.

- **Grace-based parenting:** Accepts children regardless of merit, serves children's needs without a sense of obligation, and motivates children to a higher holiness without condemnation.

- **Grace-based parents:** Joyfully recognize the God-given potential in every one of their children and sacrificially do what they can to maximize that potential for God's glory…regardless of that child's behavior.

> *But God demonstrates his own love for us in this: While we were still sinners, Christ died for us.* Romans 5:8

C. Grace-based parenting _____ the heart of God.

- He knows our deepest longings.
- He sees our truest needs.
- He understands our greatest challenges.
- He envisions our highest potential.

D. Grace-based parenting happens when we apply God's love to four key dimensions of our children's lives.

Aim Them at
True Greatness

Build Character
Into Their Heart

Atmosphere of Grace
Give Them Four Freedoms

Focus on Their
Three Inner Needs

Behold, children are a heritage from the Lord... Psalm 127:3a, NKJ

II. Parents who are fueled by God's grace have a practical, personal and powerful _____ on their kids.

A. Grace-based parenting has many benefits:

- It brings the best out of everyone involved.
- It curbs sibling rivalry.
- It empowers kids to focus in school.
- It inclines children to be a good friend and to choose their closest friends wisely.
- It guides kids when they have to deal with difficult people.
- It gives children greater respect for leadership.
- It helps kids respond positively to discipline and correction.

- It sets children up to be greater assets for the future.
- It encourages children toward choosing a gracious spouse.
- It helps children avoid extremes.
- It naturally draws children to the heart of God.

B. We need to build grace into our homes because our homes are the single most strategic influence on our _____.

Conclusion

Three steps to becoming a grace-based parent:

A. Letting God's grace into your heart. *(See appendix on page 120-121.)*

B. Letting His grace transform the way you view yourself and live your life.

C. Letting God's grace define the way you treat your children 24/7/365!

Behold, children are a heritage from the Lord… Psalm 127:3a, NKJ

Making This Yours

Getting It Started

1. What do you think your parents thought their job description was as you were raised?

2. How does your understanding of your job description as a parent differ from your parents'?

3. Based on what you see among the Christian community, what do you think the typical Christian parent thinks their job description is?

4. Is there anything about the grace-based parenting model that scares you?

5. Is there anything about the grace-based parenting model that frees you up as a parent?

Taking It Deeper

1. As you look at Luke 10:27, how does that verse translate into day-to-day living at your house? Are there any other ways you want to live out Jesus' command in that verse with your family?

> He answered: " 'Love the Lord your God with all your heart and with all your soul and with all your strength and with all your mind' ; and, 'Love your neighbor as yourself.' " Luke 10:27

2. Read Ephesians 4:29-32. How are you doing in following Paul's advice here? Is there some forgiveness needed on your part toward your parents or your child(ren)? What are you waiting for?

> Do not let any unwholesome talk come out of your mouths, but only what is helpful for building others up according to their needs, that it may benefit those who listen. And do not grieve the Holy Spirit of God, with whom you were sealed for the day of redemption. Get rid of all bitterness, rage and anger, brawling and slander, along with every form of malice. Be kind and compassionate to one another, forgiving each other, just as in Christ God forgave you. Ephesians 4: 29-32

Steps to Forgiveness

Seeking Forgiveness:

_ Admit wrongdoing without excuses.

_ Say you are sorry and mean it.

_ Ask for their forgiveness.

_ Commit to changing this behavior.

Granting Forgiveness:

_ Seek God's help.

_ Listen and accept their repentance.

_ Be generous and gracious.

_ Take the opportunity to forgive someone even if they haven't asked.

Bringing It Home

1. Look at the benefits of grace-based parenting listed below. Write each of your children's names next to at least one benefit and claim that for them. Make this a matter of prayer and an objective as you go through this study.

   A. Grace-based parenting has many benefits:

   - It brings the best out of everyone involved.
   - It curbs sibling rivalry.
   - It empowers kids to focus in school.
   - It inclines children to be a good friend and to choose their closest friends wisely.
   - It guides kids when they have to deal with difficult people.

- It gives children greater respect for leadership.
- It helps kids respond positively to discipline and correction.
- It sets children up to be greater assets for the future.
- It leans children toward choosing a gracious spouse.
- It helps children avoid extremes.
- It naturally draws children to the heart of God.

2. As Tim concluded this session, he said there were three steps to appropriating the power and presence of God's amazing grace. Where are you on each of these steps, and where would you like to be and why?

   A. The first step in becoming a grace-based parent is letting God's grace into your heart.
   Yes _____   Not Yet _____
   See the Appendix on page 120 - *How To Become A Friend Of God By Accepting His Grace.*

   B. The second step is letting His grace transform the way you see yourself and live your life. Where are you?

   (I struggle with grace)   1 2 3 4 5 6 7 8 9 1 0   (I get grace)

   What is one thing I am going to do to help myself embrace and enjoy more of God's grace?

C. The third step is letting God's grace define the way you treat your children 24/7/365! Where are you?

(I'm a beginner)   1 2 3 4 5 6 7 8 9 1 0   (Most days I am a grace-based parent)

3. As you commit to being a grace-based parent, what is one thing you are going to do this week to put into practice what you learned in this session?

Prayer:

Lord, thank you for your grace. Thank you that you love me as I am and that I don't have to earn your love. As I go through this study, please help me to love my children the way you love me – with grace. Amen

Prayer Requests:

_____

_____

_____

_____

We encourage you to read **chapter one** of Tim's book, ***Grace Based Parenting***, in order to get the most out of the upcoming session — *Why Well Meaning Parenting Falls Short*.

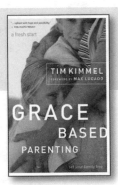

Stay Connected:
Grace Based Parenting may be a new way of thinking and acting for you. To read how others have been affected by Grace Based Parenting, go to gracebasedparenting.com.

GRACE BASED parenting
VIDEO SERIES
Creating an Atmosphere of Grace

Session 2

Why Well-Meaning Parenting Falls Short

Introduction

The job of raising great kids and enjoying the process along the way has become extremely complicated.

- Our culture _____ against us.

- Sometimes our spiritual leaders _____ us.

- Our past can _____ us.

- Our kids can _____ our best attempts.

I. **Some parents end up off course because of flawed assumptions about what it takes to groom a child for a great future.**

A. Some parents assume that kids have enough built-in _____ structure.
   – *They don't.*

B. Some parents assume _____ to a stricter and tighter standard of behavior creates safer and better kids.
   – *Not necessarily.*

C. Some parents assume raising kids in a more _____ environment helps gain more favor from God.
   – *It doesn't.*

II. **Some parents end up off course because outspoken voices within their _____ community give arbitrary parenting options an almost "biblical" priority.**

   A. Choices such as how you feed an infant, how you correct an errant child, or how you educate your child have been framed by some Christian leaders in ways that leave parents thinking that they have no other spiritual options.

   B. These narrow views of conscientious Christian parenting can cause good moms and dads to feel guilty and constantly second-guess themselves.

III. **Some parents end up off course because they are raising their children within a Christian _____.**

   A. It's hard to raise kids who develop a passion for God when they live in an environment that doesn't really need Him.

B. God has called families to serve as porch lights of faith and truth to the community around them.

You are the light of the world. A city on a hill cannot be hidden. Neither do people light a lamp and put it under a bowl. Instead they put it on its stand, and it gives light to everyone in the house. Matthew 5:14-15

C. Families committed to being lights in their community:

- Study the Bible more.
- Care for each other more.
- Reach out to hurting neighbors more.

IV. Some parents end up off course because they've adopted a _____ model of parenting.

- Fear-Based Parenting
- Image-Control Parenting
- High-Control Parenting
- Herd-Mentality Parenting
- Duct-Tape Parenting
- Life-Support or 911 Parenting

V. Grace-based parenting provides a refreshing _____ for raising kids.

Grace-based parents are a breath of fresh air because:

- They spend their time entrusting themselves to Christ
- They live to know God more
- Their children are daily recipients of the grace these parents are enjoying from the Lord
- They tend to be far more peaceful and very much in love with God
- They are especially graceful when their children are hardest to love
- They tend to be extremely grateful people
- They're seldom afraid

> *There is no fear in love. But perfect love drives out fear, because fear has to do with punishment. The one who fears is not made perfect in love. We love because he first loved us.* 1 John 4:18-19

Conclusion

Great kids don't happen by _____.

- A grace-based plan for parenting empowers parents to create an atmosphere of grace in their home by granting them four freedoms, meeting their children's true inner needs, building character into the core of their heart, and aiming them at a truly great future.

> *But grow in the grace and knowledge of our Lord and Savior Jesus Christ.*
> 2 Peter 3:18a

- Parents who want to raise truly great kids find their task so much easier and their efforts so much more rewarding when they parent their children in the power and influence of God's grace.

Making This Yours

How did you do on implementing the one practical application you committed to doing this week based on the previous session?

Getting It Started

1. Have you ever been evaluated as a parent based on the behavior of your child(ren)? When was that and how did it make you feel?

2. Have you ever been guilty of measuring another parent's effectiveness by an arbitrary standard? When?

3. Without drilling holes in a stuffed replica of your parents, which of the flawed models of parenting did your parents lean toward? How has that affected the way you parent?

    *   Fear-Based Parenting
    *   Image-Control Parenting
    *   High-Control Parenting
    *   Herd-Mentality Parenting
    *   Duct-Tape Parenting
    *   Life-Support or 911 Parenting

4. Realizing that no one is perfect, which of the flawed models of parenting are you defaulting to right now? What are some of the effects of that model on your child(ren)?

Taking It Deeper

1. Read Matthew 5:14-15. What are some of the ways that you are being a light to your community? Is/Are your child(ren) participating with you in this effort? If not, is there a way for them to be included? Or is there some other way your family can be porch lights of faith and truth to your community?

> *You are the light of the world. A city on a hill cannot be hidden. Neither do people light a lamp and put it under a bowl. Instead they put it on its stand, and it gives light to everyone in the house.* Matthew 5:14-15

2. Read Psalm 23. (You may want to read it in several translations.) List 2 or 3 ways you can see this Scripture speaking to you and your role as a parent.

3. This might be a good time to decide to forgive yourself in the areas that you feel you have fallen short. Can you do that right now? Look at 2 Corinthians 5:17. What does a "new creation" mean to you as a parent who wants to embrace grace-based parenting?

> *Therefore, if anyone is in Christ, he is a new creation; the old has gone, the new has come!* 2 Corinthians 5:17

Bringing It Home

1. As you look at the list of some of the characteristics of a grace-based home, what is attractive to you and why?

   A. Grace-based parents are a breath of fresh air because:

   - They spend their time entrusting themselves to Christ.
   - They live to know God more.
   - Their children are daily recipients of the grace these parents are enjoying from the Lord.
   - They tend to be far more peaceful and very much in love with God.
   - They are especially graceful when their children are hardest to love.
   - They tend to be extremely grateful people.
   - They're seldom afraid.

2. How has this session challenged your perceptions and/or assumptions about parenting?

3. As you commit to being a grace-based parent, what is one thing you are going to do this week to put into practice what you learned in this session?

Prayer:

Lord, I need your help to turn away from my flawed method of parenting. Please help me step out in faith and trust in you as I commit to learn to love my children the way you love me. Thank you that you have forgiven me for the mistakes I have made. Help me to forgive myself and accept your grace. Amen.

Prayer Requests:

_____

_____

_____

_____

We encourage you to read **chapter two** of Tim's book, ***Grace Based Parenting***, in order to get the most out of the upcoming session — *The Truth Behind Grace.*

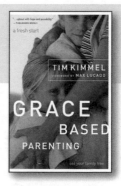

Stay Connected:

What kind of parent are you? To see what kind of parenting styles apply to you and your home, go to gracebasedparenting.com.

GRACE BASED parenting
VIDEO SERIES
Creating an Atmosphere of Grace

Session 3

The Truth Behind Grace

Introduction

Grace helps parents maintain _____ **in the midst of so many competing concerns and demands.**

    A. When a parent enforces rules with a strident and heavy hand, they tip into the discouraging style of **legalistic** parenting.

    B. When a parent takes kindness and accommodation of their children's wants to toxic levels, they tip into the debilitating style of **license-based** parenting.

    C. A grace-based home sets high standards for children without falling into the extreme traps of legalism on the one side and license on the other.

> *Grace makes it a lot easier to keep the bubble in the middle.*

    D. Grace is the ideal plan for raising truly great kids.

I. Grace-based parents avoid a _____ **attitude towards morality as well as improperly responding to a child's unique behavior.**

    A. **Legalism**

        • Legalism imposes _____ rules and man-made expectations on an equal plane with the rules and standards God outlines in the Bible.

- Legalism _____ grace.

> *Fathers, do not exasperate your children; instead, bring them up in the training and instruction of the Lord.* Ephesians 6:4

B. **License**

- License lacks clearly defined rules and standards.

- License _____ grace.

> *What shall we say, then? Shall we go on sinning so that grace may increase? By no means! We died to sin; how can we live in it any longer?* Romans 6:1–2

> *For the grace of God that brings salvation has appeared to all men. It teaches us to say, "No" to ungodliness and worldly passions, and to live self-controlled, upright and godly lives in this present age, while we wait for the blessed hope—the glorious appearing of our great God and Savior, Jesus Christ, who gave himself for us to redeem us from all wickedness and to purify for himself a people that are his very own, eager to do what is good.* Titus 2:11-14

II. Grace-based parents view their children the same way God views His.

- Grace doesn't deal with children according to their sins.
- Grace doesn't focus its attention on what is wrong with a child.
- Grace doesn't measure a child's value according to how well they adhere to a list of moral and spiritual achievements.
- Grace does not revert to condemnation, traffic in guilt, or leverage with shame.
- Grace sees children according to what they can be rather than what they can do.

III. There is an inseparable relationship between grace and

_____.

A. A truly grace-based home is one that holds up truth that is tempered by grace and practices grace that is tempered by truth.

> *In the beginning was the Word, and the Word was with God, and the Word was God…The Word became flesh and made his dwelling among us. We have seen his glory, the glory of the One, and Only who came from the Father, full of grace and truth.* John 1:1, 14

B. The graceful _____ between rules and relationship empowers parents to maintain strong moral standards without having to jeopardize their heart connection to their children.

- Rules without **relationship** lead to **rebellion**.

- Relationship without **rules** leads to **resentment**.

Conclusion

Children need parents who administer grace within the context of clearly defined biblical and moral boundaries.

- Truth is a clear light that illuminates our children's way through the dark and shadowy corridors of youth.

- Grace is the heart commitment to keep that light shining brightly no matter what.

In the same way, let your light shine before men, that they may see your good deeds and praise your Father in heaven. Matthew 5:16

Making This Yours

How did you do on implementing the one practical application you committed to doing this week based on the previous session?

Getting It Started

1. How would you characterize your upbringing – legalism or license? How did that affect your view of God? How has this affected the way you parent?

2. How have you seen the two axioms below play out in your own life or in someone else's life?

    *   Rules without **relationship** lead to **rebellion**.
    *   Relationship without **rules** leads to **resentment**.

3. Looking at the following list, how is the typical "Christian" model of parenting doing as far as loving children the way God loves His? Have you fallen into some of the traps that keep you from loving your kids this way? How?

   - Grace doesn't deal with children according to their sins.
   - Grace doesn't focus its attention on what is wrong with a child.
   - Grace doesn't measure a child's value according to how well they adhere to a list of moral and spiritual laws.
   - Grace does not revert to condemnation, traffic in guilt, or leverage with shame.
   - Grace sees children according to what they can be rather than what they can do.
   - Grace's power is in what Christ can do in children, for children, and through children.

4. If you could only have two rules in your house, what would they be? How would you graciously enforce those rules?

Taking It Deeper

1. Based on the Scripture below, does God's grace give us permission to do whatever we want? What does God's grace call us to do? What does that look like for you on a daily basis?

> *What shall we say, then? Shall we go on sinning so that grace may increase? By no means! We died to sin; how can we live in it any longer? Romans 6:1–2*

> *For the grace of God that brings salvation has appeared to all men. It teaches us to say "No" to ungodliness and worldly passions, and to live self-controlled, upright and godly lives in this present age, while we wait for the blessed hope—the glorious appearing of our great God and Savior, Jesus Christ, who gave himself for us to redeem us from all wickedness and to purify for himself a people that are his very own, eager to do what is good. Titus 2:11-14*

2. How do you think your children benefit when you live your life balancing grace and truth? What consequences have you experienced or observed when you have one but not the other (grace or truth)?

Bringing It Home

1. If grace is like a carpenter's level that shows the balance between being too strict or too lenient, what would your carpenter's level for the past 24 hours of parenting look like? Why?

2. As the saying goes, "Are you putting your money where your mouth is?" How are you personally "letting your light shine" before your child(ren) so that "they may see your good deeds and praise your Father in heaven"?

3. How has this session challenged your perceptions and/or assumptions about parenting?

4. As you commit to being a grace-based parent, what is one thing you are going to do this week to put into practice what you learned in this session?

Prayer:

Lord, thank you that you are a God of balance and you deal with us in grace and truth. I want to do the same for my children. Help me not to fall into the traps of legalism or license as I represent your love to my children. Lord, would you please give me your wisdom as I try to overcome the hang-ups of my own upbringing and balance between the rules of our home and the relationships with which I have been entrusted? I love you Lord. Thank you for your guidance. Amen.

Prayer Requests:

_____

_____

_____

_____

We encourage you to read **chapter three** of Tim's book, ***Grace Based Parenting***, in order to get the most out of the upcoming session — *A Secure Love.*

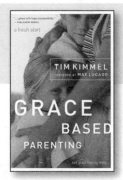

Stay Connected:

This session addresses one of the main sticking points when it comes to embracing Grace Based Parenting. For a comprehensive explanation of grace and truth, go to gracebasedparenting.com.

GRACE BASED
parenting
VIDEO SERIES
Creating an Atmosphere of Grace

Session 4

A Secure Love

Aim Them at True Greatness

Build Character
Into Their Hearts

Four Freedoms

Three Inner Needs

Secure
Love

Introduction

All children long for a love that is secure.

    A.   Every child is born with three fundamental, driving inner needs: **True Needs**.

        1.   A need for *security*

        2.   A need for *significance*

        3.   A need for *strength*

        Go to www.gracebasedparenting.com to see how Satan appealed to these needs in a counterfeit way.

    B.   Grace-based parents equip their children for a much more effective and meaningful future when they use each day to give their children:

        1.   A Secure __________________

        2.   A Significant ________________

        3.   A Strong _________________

    C.   Every word you say, every decision, and every ________________ is an opportunity to meet these three true needs.

Dear friends, let us love one another, for love comes from God. Everyone who loves has been born of God and knows God. Whoever does not love does not know God, because God is love. This is how God showed his love among us: He sent his one and only Son into the world that we might live through him. This is love: not that we loved God, but that he loved us and sent his Son as an atoning sacrifice for our sins. Dear friends, since God so loved us, we also ought to love one another.
1 John 4:7-11

I. Many children have a difficult time gaining secure love from their parents because that love is _____.

  A. Some children feel that they have to _____ for their parent's love.

  B. Some children feel that they have to _____ their parent's love.

  C. It's much easier to transfer a secure love to our child's heart if we work from a clear _____ of love.

> *Love is the commitment of my will to your needs and best interests, regardless of the cost.*

II. There are three powerful ways to build a secure love into a child's heart.

    A. We need to _____ them as they are.

        1. Children feel accepted when we appreciate the things about them over which they have no control:

- Their gender
- Their IQ
- Their mannerisms
- Their learning styles

- Their physical features
- Their physical abilities
- Their emotional capacities

        2. We accept our children when we model the same endearing love that Jesus had.

Let the children alone, and do not hinder them from coming to Me; for the kingdom of heaven belongs to such as these. Matthew 19:14, NASB

    B. We need to make sure they know they are _____ with a loving and honoring home.

        1. Homes of honor see each child's time, skills, and dreams as gifts to be cherished and stewarded carefully.

        2. Homes of honor still have room for sibling rivalry and occasional disappointments, but for the most part, these are homes that show respect for a child's uniqueness and vulnerabilities.

The righteous man leads a blameless life; blessed are his children after him. Proverbs 20:7

C. We need to give them regular and generous helpings of

_____.

1. Every child was born to respond to meaningful touch.

2. The hugs and kisses that children receive from their parents become a reservoir of security in their hearts.

3. Both boys and girls need affection from both their mother and their father.

> *Taking a child, he set him before them, and **taking him in His arms**, He said to them, "Whoever receives one child **like this** in My name receives Me…"* Mark 9:36-37a, NASB (emphasis added)

Conclusion

A secure love prepares them for a future of true greatness.

- Satan would love to help your children gain their sense of inner security from counterfeits like popularity and applause.

- Grace-based parents transfer a secure love to their children by accepting them as they are, creating a loving and honoring spirit within their home, and giving them generous helpings of affection.

> *Above all, love each other deeply, because love covers over a multitude of sins. Offer hospitality to one another without grumbling. Each one should use whatever gift he has received to serve others, faithfully administering God's grace in its various forms.* 1 Peter 4:8-10

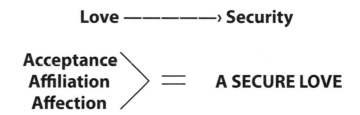

Making This Yours

How did you do this past week implementing the one practical application you committed to in the previous session?

Getting It Started

1. How has the lack or presence of a secure love in your life affected who you are today?

2. What would your child(ren) say they are competing against for your love and attention?

3. How may you have inadvertently given your kids the impression that they have to do certain things to earn your love?

4. What part of Tim's definition of love is hardest for you to carry out? Why?

"Love is the commitment of my will"

"To your needs and best interests"

"Regardless of the cost"

Taking It Deeper

1. Based on 1 John 4:7-11, we should be compelled to love others because of God's great love for us. What are some of the ways God loves you that motivate you to love others in the same way?

> *Dear friends, let us love one another, for love comes from God. Everyone who loves has been born of God and knows God. Whoever does not love does not know God, because God is love. This is how God showed his love among us: He sent his one and only Son into the world that we might live through him. This is love: not that we loved God, but that he loved us and sent his Son as an atoning sacrifice for our sins. Dear friends, since God so loved us, we also ought to love one another.*
> 1 John 4:7-11

2. As you look at the verses in Mark below, put your child in Jesus' arms. How should you be receiving and loving your child like Jesus is?

> *Taking a child, he set him before them, and **taking him in His arms**, He said to them, "Whoever receives one child **like this** in My name receives Me…"*
> Mark 9:36-37a NASB, (emphasis added)

Bringing It Home

1. When it comes to instilling a secure love into your children, Tim says they feel secure when we accept the things about them over which they have no control. As you look at the list below, put your child's name next to the area(s) that you need to work on accepting in them. Next to their name, put a specific action you will take to convey your acceptance.

   - Their gender –

   - Their IQ –

   - Their mannerisms –

   - Their learning styles –

   - Their physical features –

   - Their physical abilities –

   - Their emotional capacities –

2. How are you doing at giving regular and generous helpings of affection to your child(ren)? List each of your children below. Next to their name put a new or more abundant way you are going to communicate a secure love to them through godly, meaningful affection.

- _____ –

- _____ –

- _____ –

- _____ –

- _____ –

3. How has this session challenged your perceptions and/or assumptions about parenting?

4. As you commit to being a grace-based parent, what is one thing you are going to do this week to put into practice what you have learned in this session?

Bonus Section for Single Parents, Blended Families, and Other Unique Family Configurations

1. As a single parent or step-parent, it can be very tempting to try to compete with an ex-spouse for the love of your child. In doing so, you may be undermining a secure love in your child(ren). If you are doing this, how can you rise above it and make sure you are making deposits of acceptance and affection into your child's heart?

2. Because sibling rivalry can be heightened when there is added stress in a family, what can you do to make sure you encourage honor, rather than dishonor, among your family members?

Prayer:

Lord, thank you that you love us with an unconditional love – there is nothing we can do to earn your love or make you love us more. As I commit to being a grace-based parent, help me to instill that kind of secure love into the heart of my child(ren). Forgive me for the ways I have fallen short, and thank you so much that love can cover a multitude of mistakes. Amen.

Prayer Requests:

_____

_____

_____

_____

We encourage you to read **chapter four** of Tim's book, ***Grace Based Parenting***, in order to get the most out of the upcoming session — *A Significant Purpose.*

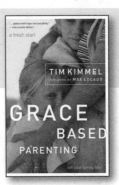

Stay Connected:
For some very practical ways to give your child a secure love, go to www.gracebasedparenting.com.

GRACE BASED parenting
VIDEO SERIES
Creating an Atmosphere of Grace

Session 5

A Significant Purpose

Aim Them at True Greatness

Build Character
Into Their Hearts

Four Freedoms

Three Inner Needs

Secure Love | Significant Purpose

Introduction

All children need to know they have a significant purpose on earth.

A. There is a deep longing in the heart of every child to make a
_____.

> *Although many people can contribute to the process of creating a significant purpose, it is a child's parents that carry the greatest potential for influence.*

B. Parents need to have a deliberate and gracious involvement in identifying and developing _____.

I. **Children have four levels of purpose that need to be developed.**

A. A _____ Purpose

> *A general purpose empowers a child to grow up to play a strategic role in the larger family of mankind.*

> *Do nothing out of selfish ambition or vain conceit, but in humility consider others better than yourselves. Each of you should look not only to your own interests, but also to the interest of others.* Philippians 2:3-4

B.   A _____ Purpose

> *A specific purpose enables a child to use their God-given skills and abilities wisely.*

C.   A _____ Purpose

> *A relational purpose allows a child to navigate his or her social context in a much more deliberate and valuable way.*

D.   A _____ Purpose

> *A spiritual purpose helps a child develop a meaningful and eternal relationship with God, as well as prepares them to make a spiritual difference in other people's lives.*

> *You are the salt of the earth… You are the light of the world… let your light shine before men, that they may see your good deeds and praise your Father in heaven.* Matthew 5:13,14,16

A Significant Purpose

II. There are three powerful ways to build a significant purpose into a child's heart.

A. Give them regular _____.

- Kids who hear well-timed affirmation from their parents are more easily convinced of their God-given intrinsic worth.

- Affirmation loves to catch children doing things right. It notices when they do things that don't come easily to them.

- We must avoid the trap of handing out a lot of empty praise.

    I praise you, for I am fearfully and wonderfully made. Wonderful are your works; my soul knows it very well.
    Psalm 139:14, ESV

B. Give them focused _____.

- It's hard to build a significant purpose into people who feel like footnotes to our daily lives.

C. Give them graceful _____.

- Everyone is born with a bent toward selfishness. The lure of sin loses a lot of its potency when a life of grace is attractively modeled.

- When our children fall short, discipline and consequences—applied with grace—communicate the incredible worth we place on them.

> *It is for discipline that you endure; God deals with you as with sons; for what son is there whom his father does not discipline? ... Furthermore, we had earthly fathers to discipline us, and we respected them; shall we not much rather be subject to the Father of spirits and live? ... All discipline for the moment seems not to be joyful, but sorrowful; yet to those who have been trained by it, afterwards it yields the peaceful fruit of righteousness.* Hebrews 12:7, 9, 11, NASB

Conclusion

It's never too late.

- We matter more to our kids than we realize. They were born with a need to make a difference. For good or for ill, we play the biggest role in determining what kind of difference they will ultimately make.

- Grace-based parents transfer a significant purpose to their children by giving them regular affirmation, focused attention, and graceful admonition.

Purpose ———→ Significance

Affirmation
Attention 〉 = **A SIGNIFICANT PURPOSE**
Admonition

Making This Yours

How did you do this past week implementing the one practical application you committed to in the previous session?

Getting It Started

1. What did you dream of growing up to be when you were a child? Is reality anywhere close to those dreams? What part did your parents play in where you are today?

2. How are you doing modeling to your children the general life purpose of developing the potential of as many people as you can? Have you been rewarded with evidence of your child(ren) grasping this purpose yet?

3. At what stage is/are each of your child(ren) in embracing a spiritual purpose? As you honestly share, enlist others to pray for your child(ren) on their spiritual journey.

4. Name your child(ren)'s three best friends, favorite subject in school, their favorite sports team, and musical group. How are you doing at paying attention to the things that matter to them?

Taking It Deeper

1. In Matthew 25:21, we see the value of encouraging and developing the gifts that God entrusts to us. List each of your children and put down at least two skills, talents, or attributes that you are committed to nurturing in them for God's glory.

> *….Well done, good and faithful servant! You have been faithful with a few things; I will put you in charge of many things.* Matthew 25:21

2. The Scripture below reminds us that discipline is a form of grace, and we communicate significance and worth when we gracefully admonish our children. What is the difference between discipline and punishment? How are you doing at administering discipline and consequences gracefully (the way God deals with us)? How can you improve?

> *It is for discipline that you endure; God deals with you as with sons; for what son is there whom his father does not discipline? ... Furthermore, we had earthly fathers to discipline us, and we respected them; shall we not much rather be subject to the Father of spirits and live? ... All discipline for the moment seems not to be joyful, but sorrowful; yet to those who have been trained by it, afterwards it yields the peaceful fruit of righteousness.* Hebrews 12:7, 9, 11, NASB

Bringing It Home

1. How are you doing at giving legitimate praise to your children? Are you too stingy or too insincere? If so, come up with two ways you can make your affirmation count more toward instilling a significant purpose into the heart of your child(ren).

2. Would your children say that they have your focused attention when they need it? In what ways can you become more available to your children, and use those times of attention to reinforce their incredible worth and significance?

3. How has this session challenged your perceptions and/or assumptions about parenting?

4. As you commit to being a grace-based parent, what is one thing you are going to do this week to put into practice what you have learned in this session?

Prayer:

Dear Lord, thank you that you give our life eternal significance and that you have a divine purpose of each of our lives. Help us communicate the incredible worth that you have placed on each of our children by what we say, what we do, and how we do it. It is our greatest desire to see our children grasp their spiritual purpose. Thank you that you use us as part of that journey. Amen.

Prayer Requests:

_____

_____

_____

_____

We encourage you to read **chapter five** of Tim's book, ***Grace Based Parenting***, in order to get the most out of the upcoming session — *A Strong Hope*.

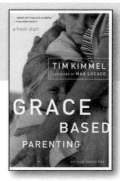

Stay Connected:

For some very practical ways to give your child a significant purpose, go to www.gracebasedparenting.com.

GRACE BASED parenting

VIDEO SERIES

Creating an Atmosphere of Grace

Session 6

A Strong Hope

Aim Them at True Greatness

Build Character Into Their Hearts

Four Freedoms

Three Inner Needs

Secure Love | Significant Purpose | Strong Hope

Introduction

All children need to know they have a strong hope for the future.

    A.   Parents who are deliberate about meeting their children's inner need for strength make it easier for their kids to:

- Grow up to be visionaries.
- Trust in a better future.
- Long for a greater good.
- Ultimately put their hope in God.

    B.   Parents who model a strong trust in God _____ a confident hope into the deepest recesses of a child's heart.

I.   God provides unique dynamics of youth that lend themselves to transferring a strong hope into a child.

    A.   Our children's sense of hope is strengthened when we enthusiastically and sacrificially care for them during those years in their lives when they are primarily _____.

- Children develop a strong hope when they can rely on their parents to lovingly and reliably meet their physical and emotional needs.

> *Therefore I tell you, do not worry about your life, what you will eat or drink; or about your body, what you will wear…But seek first his kingdom and his righteousness, and all these things will be given to you as well.* Matthew 6:25, 33

B. Our children's sense of hope is strengthened when we willingly start to hand over responsibility for their lives.

1. There are two extreme views of helping children that undermine their ability to develop a strong hope:

   a) Hardly helping them at all.
   b) Continuing to help them when they are really ready (and would prefer) to stand on their own two feet.

> *Until we all reach unity in the faith and in the knowledge of the Son of God and become mature, attaining to the whole measure of the fullness of Christ. Then we will no longer be infants, tossed back and forth by the waves, and blown here and there by every wind of teaching and by the cunning and craftiness of men in their deceitful scheming. Instead, speaking the truth in love, we will in all things grow up into him who is the Head, that is, Christ.* Ephesians 4:13-15

2. Grace-based parents know the balance between **protecting** their children in their helplessness and **preparing** their children for independence.

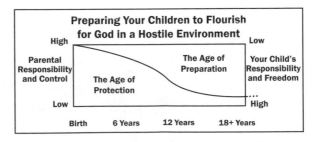

from Dr. Kimmel's book, *Why Christian Kids Rebel*, page 195.

II. There are three powerful ways to build a strong hope into a child's heart.

A. Children develop a strong hope when they know their parents recognize their God-given _____ and turn them into assets for the future.

> *Train a child in the way he should go, and when he is old he will not turn from it.* Proverbs 22:6

B. Children develop a strong hope when their parents lead them and encourage them to live a great spiritual _____.

1. Many parents preoccupy themselves with raising _____ children.

2. Kids raised in "safe" Christian environments can become:

   - Spiritually lazy.
   - Overly critical of people caught in the traps of the world system.
   - Naïve about the world system to the point that they can be easily programmed by it once they are out on their own.
   - Indifferent.

3. Grace-based parents don't make it their aim to raise safe kids. Instead, they want to raise _____ kids.

> *Now faith is being sure of what we hope for and certain of what we do not see.* Hebrews 11:1

C. Children develop a strong hope when their parents help them turn their childhood into a series of positive _____.

1. Grace-based parents show their children how to:

   • Work hard.
   • Get along with difficult people.
   • Solve confusing problems.
   • Handle money.
   • Repent.
   • Forgive.
   • Fear God a lot.
   • Fear their fellow man very little.
   • Laugh and cry at the right time.
   • Bring the best out of the people closest to them.

2. Childhood provides ample time to give children outlets to turn these ingredients from "nice tries" into proven accomplishments that strengthen their sense of hope for the future.

Conclusion

A strong hope prepares our children for a future of true greatness.

A. Grace-based parents transfer a strong hope to their children by:

- Turning their unique, God-given abilities into assets.

- Leading the way in living a great spiritual adventure.

- Working to turn both their victories and defeats into a series of positive accomplishments.

Hope ——————→ Strength

Abilities
Adventure ⟩ = **A STRONG HOPE**
Accomplishments

Making This Yours

How did you do this past week implementing the one practical application you committed to in the previous session?

Getting It Started

1. What things in your upbringing gave you a feeling of strength and sufficiency when you grew up?

2. Does the idea of raising strong kids instead of raising safe kids scare you? Why do you think this is? What is one spiritual adventure you can experience with your child(ren)?

3. What are you doing to keep your children helpless by over-protecting them rather than preparing them? What is one thing you will do to change this?

4. Are there areas of challenge in your child's life that you wish God would remove (i.e. physical, intellectual, emotional, relational or professional)? Have you been able to see how this challenge has encouraged you and your child to place your hope in the goodness of God? If so, how?

5. When your child faces his or her next setback or failure, what will you do to turn it into an opportunity to build a strong hope?

Taking It Deeper

1. 2 Corinthians 12:9-10 gives a different perspective on weaknesses and encourages us to turn them into a dependence on God. How are you doing with modeling this to your child(ren)? How are you submitting your weaknesses to God and relying on His power? Can you think of one way you can allow your weakness to point to a mighty God?

> *My grace is sufficient for you, for my power is made perfect in weakness. Therefore I will boast all the more gladly about my weaknesses, so that Christ's power may rest on me. That is why, for Christ's sake, I delight in weaknesses, in insults, in hardships, in persecutions, in difficulties. For when I am weak, then I am strong.* 2 Corinthians 12:9-10

2. As you read these inspiring words from Isaiah, how have you personally experienced God renewing your strength as you hope in Him?

> *He gives strength to the weary and increases the power of the weak. Even youths grow tired and weary, and young men stumble and fall; but those who hope in the LORD will renew their strength. They will soar on wings like eagles; they will run and not grow weary, they will walk and not be faint.* Isaiah 40:29-31

Bringing It Home

1. Tim talks about turning our child's God-given abilities into assets for the future and helping them turn their childhood into a series of positive accomplishments.

> *Write these commandments that I've given you today on your hearts. Get them inside of you and then get them inside your children. Talk about them wherever you are, sitting at home or walking in the street; talk about them from the time you get up in the morning to when you fall into bed at night.* Deuteronomy 6:6-7, The Message

Building a strong hope into our child(ren) is much more likely to bring the best out of them when we are deliberate about preparing them for independence from us and dependence on God. Below is a progression of moving from protection to preparation.
Using the list below, put your child's name next to the stage you are most using with them. Should you be moving toward the next stage in some training?

How are you doing on the admonishments of micro-managing and praising?

- If their maturity level or ability is low:
  Direct them (show them how).

- If their maturity or ability is medium:
  Develop them (ask questions; help them figure it out).

- If their maturity or ability is high:
  Delegate to them (let them try it their way; help them learn from their mistakes).

  * **Don't micromanage them.**
  * **Do praise them.**

2. How has this session challenged your perceptions and/or assumptions about parenting?

3. As you commit to being a grace-based parent, what is one thing you are going to do this week to put into practice what you have learned in this session?

Prayer:

Lord, thank you so much for the hope that we have for today and tomorrow in you. We are humbled by our privilege of passing that hope on to our child(ren). Please help me as I model a strong trust and dependence on you. I pray that as my children see me depending upon you for courage and strength, they will be inspired to do the same. Please give me your wisdom as I prepare my children for a future with a strong hope. Amen.

Prayer Requests:

_____

_____

_____

_____

We encourage you to read **chapters six and seven** of Tim's book, ***Grace Based Parenting***, in order to get the most out of the upcoming session — *The Freedom to be Different*.

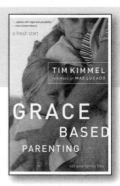

Stay Connected:

For some very practical ways to give your child a strong hope, go to www.gracebasedparenting.com.

GRACE BASED parenting

VIDEO SERIES

Creating an Atmosphere of Grace

Session 7

The Freedom To Be Different

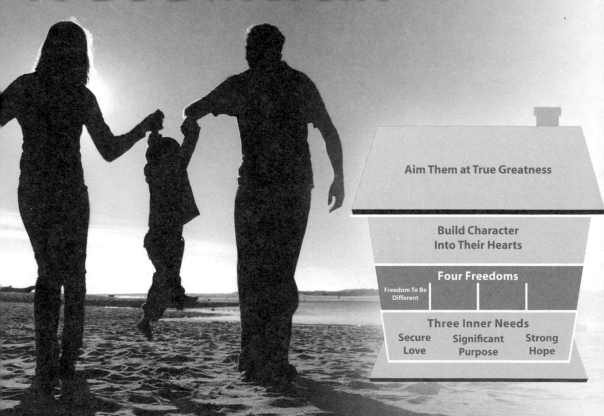

Aim Them at True Greatness

Build Character
Into Their Hearts

Four Freedoms

Freedom To Be Different

Three Inner Needs

Secure
Love

Significant
Purpose

Strong
Hope

Introduction

Children are far more inclined to align their lives with God if they are raised in an _____ that reflects the heart of His grace.

A. A grace-based home consistently communicates a love that isn't determined by a child's behavior.

> *For as high as the heavens are above the earth, so great is his love for those who fear him…As a father has compassion on his children, so the LORD has compassion on those who fear him; for he knows how we are formed, he remembers that we are dust…But from everlasting to everlasting the LORD'S love is with those who fear him, and his righteousness with their children's children.* Psalm 103:11,13-14,17

B. An atmosphere of grace in our home encourages parents to:

- Listen more and lecture less.
- Respond more and react less.
- Engage more and dismiss less.
- Pray more and judge less.

C. A grace-based home doesn't _____ minor issues or elevate non-essentials out of proportion.

I. **The first way parents can create an atmosphere of grace is to give children the freedom to be _____.**

    A. "Different" in this context refers to attitudes and actions that are weird, bizarre, strange, goofy, or quirky but not necessarily _____.

        1. Legalistic patterns of parenting emphasize the _____ of Christian behavior over the substance of Christian living.

        2. Fear-based parenting grants more power and influence to the external forces of the world system than it does to the _____ power and presence of God.

> *Greater is He who is in you than he who is in the world.*
> 1 John 4:4, NASB

    B. It is very easy to react to our children's "different" behavior because:

- It annoys us.
- It embarrasses us.
- We jump to the conclusion that what they are doing is wrong.

II. **Grace-based parents are careful not to make arbitrary standards and expectations _____ issues.**

    A. Grace-based parents avoid the trap of using the _____ to justify their personal preferences.

B. When a parent uses the Bible to speak out against a child that is "different" but not necessarily doing anything biblically wrong, that parent may be using the Lord's name in vain.

> *You shall not misuse the name of the LORD your God, for the LORD will not hold anyone guiltless who misuses his name.* Exodus 20:7

C. Children are more inclined to respect and respond to a parent's rules when they are:

- Established in an atmosphere of grace.
- Reasonable and logical.

III. Some "different" behavior might have its source in a genuine problem within the child's _____.

A. Some "different" behavior is simply a child's strength pushed to an extreme.

- Grace-based parenting focuses on tempering the behavior without condemning or squelching it.

B. Some "different" behavior is an outward expression of an inward
_____ with sin, anger, or shame.

- Grace-based parents focus their attention on connecting with the heart of the child rather than attacking the external manifestation of their internal problems.

- When the internal problem is corrected, the outside tends to take care of itself.

Conclusion

Giving children the freedom to be different sets them up to harness so much more of their God-given _____.

- Grace gives children the freedom to be unique.

- Giving children the freedom to be different communicates an unconditional love and an intrinsic worth that is at the heart of God's amazing grace.

Making This Yours

How did you do on implementing the one practical application you committed to doing this week based on the previous session?

Getting It Started

1. What sort of things (not evil or sinful) did you do as a teenager that annoyed your parents? How did they react?

2. What are some of the ways that your child(ren) are different, quirky, bizarre, or unique? Have you been annoyed or embarrassed by these?

3. Why do you think we have a tendency to attach evil power to things or actions? How have you observed the Christian community doing this? What are some of the outcomes of this fallacy?

4. What are some of the ways we judge other parents based on the behavior of their child(ren)?

Taking It Deeper

1. As you look at the verses below that tell us how we are to love each other, which of these qualities of love makes it easier to give our child(ren) the freedom to be different?

> *Love is patient, love is kind. It does not envy, it does not boast, it is not proud. It is not rude, it is not self-seeking, it is not easily angered, it keeps no record of wrongs. Love does not delight in evil but rejoices with the truth. It always protects, always trusts, always hopes, always perseveres.*
> 1 Corinthians 13:4-7

2. How does the verse below change the way you view the external forces of the world system? Does it encourage fear or faith?

> *You, dear children, are from God and have overcome them, because the one who is in you is greater than the one who is in the world.* 1 John 4:4

Bringing It Home

1. The next time your child(ren) wants to follow a fad, what are you going to do? A few hints: Is it a biblical or moral issue? Is it a practical or financial issue? Is it a personal issue with you or them?

2. How can we come alongside other parents who are struggling with their child(ren) and be an asset rather than a detractor?

3. How has this session challenged your perceptions and/or assumptions about parenting?

4. As you commit to being a grace-based parent, what is one thing you are going to do this week to put into practice what you learned in this session?

Bonus Section for Single Parents, Blended Families, and Other Unique Family Configurations

1. Am I doing what I can to remove residue from the past that is distracting me from carrying out the principles of this session? What am I going to do about this?

2. When it comes to applying the principles of this session, how am I going to deal with the unique difficulties in my family that are brought on by:

   - Fatigue
   - Finances
   - Guilt
   - Anger
   - Regret
   - Children's suffering

3. Regarding this session, who can I count on to come alongside of me with encouragement and assistance? How am I going to communicate my needs?

Prayer:

> *Dear Lord, thank you for the child(ren) you have placed under my care. Would you please help me celebrate the ways you have made these child(ren) unique? Help me see what you see in them and not look at them through the critical eyes of others. Give me patience as my children express their weird behavior and help me love them the way you love me – with grace. Amen.*

Prayer Requests:

_____

_____

_____

_____

We encourage you to read **chapter eight** of Tim's book, ***Grace Based Parenting***, in order to get the most out of the upcoming session — *The Freedom to be Vulnerable.*

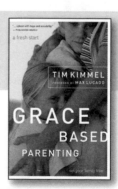

Stay Connected:

Do you ever wish your kids came with instructions? It might be easier to understand their weird behavior and accept their differences if they did. Well we've got good news! *The Kids Flag Page* is the operating manual that should have come with your child.

Don't wait any longer to discover who God made your child to be, what motivates them and how to tailor your parenting to their unique inner bent.

Go to www.gracebasedparenting.com to watch a video and find out more about this fun, eye-opening tool.

GRACE BASED
parenting
VIDEO SERIES
Creating an Atmosphere of Grace

Session 8

The Freedom To Be Vulnerable

Aim Them at True Greatness

Build Character Into Their Hearts

Four Freedoms

| Freedom To Be Different | Freedom To Be Vulnerable | | |

Three Inner Needs

| Secure Love | Significant Purpose | Strong Hope |

Introduction

A grace-based home provides the ideal atmosphere for children to process the fragile nature of youth.

A. Grace-based parents make it their aim to consistently communicate an affirming and accepting love – especially during the awkward periods of childhood.

B. Grace-based parents offer a safe haven for a child's transparent heart.

C. Grace-based parenting extends to our children the same _____ _____ that God extends to His children.

> But he gives us more grace. That is why Scripture says: "God opposes the proud but gives grace to the humble." James 4:6

> Let us then approach the throne of grace with confidence, so that we may receive mercy and find grace to help in our time of need. Hebrews 4:16

I. **The second way parents can create an atmosphere of grace is to give children the freedom to be** _____.

    A. Children are born with an unsophisticated set of emotions.

        1. They are prone to vast mood swings, vain imaginations, and inordinate fears.

        2. They need parents who don't overreact, trivialize, or write them off.

> *Cast all your anxiety on him because he cares for you.* 1 Peter 5:7

    B. Home must be a place where children don't have to wear _____ over their emotions.

    C. Children need to know that they can voice their feelings and discuss their inadequacies without fear of them being _____ .

II. **Grace-based parents help their children process the tension between the facts of a given situation and the feelings that might be distorting those facts.**

    A. It's not uncommon for children's feelings about a given situation to have no _____ whatsoever to the facts.

        1. The lack of maturity that surrounds childhood often makes it difficult for kids to see beyond their emotions.

2. Healthy adults are people who adequately process their feelings but make their decisions based on truth, facts, logic, and

_____   _____.

3. Grace-based parents carefully help children process their vulnerabilities so that they aren't ultimately defined or mastered by their emotions.

B. Children need an atmosphere of grace that offers:

- Love instead of lectures
- Understanding instead of ignorance
- Compassion instead of dismissal

III. One of the best ways to help children process their vulnerabilities is by meeting their three driving inner needs.

A. It's much easier for children to learn to face their fears and move beyond their embarrassments when they have been given a deep sense of security, a significance purpose, and a strong hope.

> "My grace is sufficient for you, for my power is made perfect in weakness." Therefore I will boast all the more gladly about my weaknesses, so that Christ's power may rest on me. That is why, for Christ's sake, I delight in weaknesses, in insults, in hardships, in persecutions, in difficulties. For when I am weak, then I am strong.
> 2 Corinthians 12:9-10

B. The best way to help kids gracefully deal with their vulnerabilities is by letting them see their mother and/or father trusting in God's secure love, significant purpose, and strong hope through the difficulties and fears they face as adults.

Conclusion

Giving children the freedom to be vulnerable allows them to safely voice their fears and share their inadequacies with their parents.

- Grace-based parents handle their children's vulnerabilities with respect.

- Grace-based parents avoid trivializing their children's fears or emotions.

Making This Yours

How did you do on implementing the one practical application you committed to doing this week based on the previous session?

Getting It Started

1. What were some of your childhood vulnerabilities (height, weight, social status, athletic aptitude)? Was there someone in your life whose encouragement during a very vulnerable moment changed the way you view yourself?

2. What emotional situations in your child(ren)'s lives are you tempted to trivialize? If we are responding to them the way God responds to us, how should we handle them?

3. Do you or your child(ren) have a "thorn in the flesh" that will probably never be taken away? How have you dealt with this or how will you help your child(ren) accept and make the most of theirs?

4. Has there been a time when you have modeled to your child(ren) a secure love, a significant purpose, and a strong hope in God by how you have trusted Him in a very vulnerable situation?

Taking It Deeper

1. What is it about God and His love that encourages us to approach His throne of grace with confidence? How are we transferring that boldness to our children?

   Let us then approach the throne of grace with confidence, so that we may receive mercy and find grace to help us in our time of need. Hebrews 4:16

2. How have you seen God's strength made perfect in your weakness? Have you been able to actually delight in your hardships, persecutions or difficulties? What is it about God's strength that may be able to help you delight in your weaknesses? How can you improve?

   But he said to me, "My grace is sufficient for you, for my power is made perfect in weakness." Therefore I will boast all the more gladly about my weaknesses, so that Christ's power may rest on me. That is why, for Christ's sake, I delight in weaknesses, in insults, in hardships, in persecutions, in difficulties. For when I am weak, then I am strong. 2 Corinthians 12:9-10

Bringing It Home

1. Think of a very vulnerable situation that your child(ren) may some day find themselves in. How could you love them with grace during this time?

2. Take a moment to think about one or two ways you can encourage your child(ren) right now as they make their way through the vulnerable time of childhood. As you share these with the group, pray for one another and hold each other accountable to do them.

3. How has this session challenged your perceptions and/or assumptions about parenting?

4. As you commit to being a grace-based parent, what is one thing you are going to do this week to put into practice what you learned in this session?

Bonus Section for Single Parents, Blended Families, and Other Unique Family Configurations

1. Am I doing what I can to remove residue from the past that is distracting me from carrying out the principles of this session? What am I going to do about this?

2. When it comes applying the principles of this session, how am I going to deal with the unique difficulties in my family that are brought on by:

    - Fatigue
    - Finances
    - Guilt
    - Anger
    - Regret
    - Children's suffering

3. Regarding this session, who can I count on to come alongside of me with encouragement and assistance? How am I going to communicate my needs?

Prayer:

Lord, you know our hearts and how we suffer during times of hurt, disappointment and embarrassment. Thank you that you are always there with your unconditional love. As we give our child(ren) the freedom to be vulnerable, help us to be a safe haven for their emotions and feelings. Keep us from trivializing the hard things they are going through in their young lives. We pray that our love for them will point them to You. Amen.

Prayer Requests:

_____

_____

_____

_____

We encourage you to read **chapter nine** of Tim's book, ***Grace Based Parenting***, in order to get the most out of the upcoming session — *The Freedom to be Candid.*

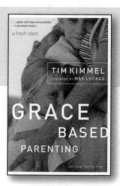

Stay Connected:

Our kids need our love more than ever when they are feeling vulnerable. For some fresh ideas on how to really love your kids, go to www.gracebasedparenting.com.

GRACE BASED parenting

VIDEO SERIES

Creating an Atmosphere of Grace

Session 9

The Freedom To Be Candid

Aim Them at True Greatness

Build Character
Into Their Hearts

Four Freedoms

Freedom To Be
Different | Freedom To Be
Vulnerable | Freedom To Be
Candid

Three Inner Needs

Secure
Love | Significant
Purpose | Strong
Hope

Introduction

Truthfulness and forthrightness are supposed to be anchor tenants of an atmosphere of grace.

    A. Because people tend to communicate the uncomfortable issues within relationships from the platform of their feelings, graciousness is often forced out of the picture.

    B. To keep this from happening, grace-based families need a brand of honesty that consistently frames painful truth in a way that helps rather than harms. Candor is that brand of honesty.

    C. There is a high degree of fairness brought to bear within the true meaning of *candor*.

I.   The third way parents can create an atmosphere of grace is to give children the freedom to be _____.

    A. Candor allows for a verbal give-and-take between parents and a child that promotes honesty dipped in _____.

        1. A grace-based atmosphere works to create a careful forthrightness that guards the other person's dignity.

        2. A grace-based atmosphere encourages children to talk about the deep, and sometimes troubling, issues they are working through in a way that builds them up and makes them better people.

> *...continue to work out your salvation with fear and trembling.*
> Philippians 2:12b

B. Candor provides a safe forum in which children can air their doubts, disappointments, and even their misguided _____.

   1. During these times, children need parents who _____ _____ and spend time on their knees.

   2. Running truth through a filter of love moves honesty to the more _____-_____ level of candor.

   3. If the family atmosphere is dominated by grace, children will not be defined by their struggles and controlled by the powers of darkness.

      • **Strident, legalistic homes** set children up to be critical.

      • **Fear-based families** set children up to be intimidated by life.

      • **Lawless homes** set children up to be dishonoring and self-absorbed.

> *Fathers, do not exasperate your children; instead, bring them up in the training and instruction of the Lord.* Ephesians 6:4

   4. Grace-based parents _____ their children to openly and respectfully share their opinions.

II. Grace requires that we exchange words about touchy subjects with a commitment to help – even heal – the other person.

    A. We need to create an easy way for them to voice the cries of their hearts so we can help them process issues adequately.

        1. Grace makes room for children to tell their parents things about themselves that parents might not be excited to hear.

        2. Grace makes room for children to walk with their parents through adult issues they are struggling with such as sex, substance abuse, or spiritual doubts.

        3. Grace makes room for children to tell parents frustrations they are having with them as parents.

        4. The best way to ensure that our children will speak respectfully to us is to make sure that we speak respectfully when we are voicing our disappointment with them.

> *See to it that no one misses the grace of God and that no bitter root grows up to cause trouble and defile many.* Hebrews 12:15

> *Let your conversation be always full of grace, seasoned with salt, so that you may know how to answer everyone.* Colossians 4:6

Conclusion

Children brought up in grace-based homes have the freedom to be candid and enjoy a comfortable and easy outlet of communication with their parents.

- Regardless of age, children need to know that they can communicate the deepest struggles within their hearts without worrying about it costing them in the future.

- Allowing kids to be respectfully candid with their parents sets them up to enjoy an adulthood without regrets.

To find out how to have your own "What's Your Beef Night", go to www.gracebasedparenting.com.

Making This Yours

How did you do on implementing the one practical application you committed to doing this week based on the previous session?

Getting It Started

1. Have you ever been the victim of toxic honesty? How did it make you feel?

2. Why does it make us nervous as parents when our child(ren) voice(s) doubts about their spiritual convictions? What does our anxiety say about our view of the Holy Spirit?

3. What are some of the messages we communicate to our child(ren) when we respond to their candor with high control, belittling, bullying, or triteness? What can we do that will encourage them to approach us again in candor?

4. If a colleague or friend disagreed with you, how would you want them to handle the disagreement?

Taking It Deeper

1. How do you think fathers and mothers exasperate their child(ren) when it comes to the give, take, and honor that is supposed to be associated with candor? What are some ways that you can instruct and train a child without reacting, controlling, or intimidating?

    Fathers, do not exasperate your children; instead, bring them up in the training and instruction of the Lord. Ephesians 6:4

2. Have you ever had a heated discussion with God, similar to the one Moses had referenced below? What was the outcome? How did that affect your faith?

> *"I have seen these people," the Lord said to Moses, "and they are a stiff-necked people. Now leave me alone so that my anger may burn against them and that I may destroy them." But Moses sought the favor of the Lord his God…"Turn from your fierce anger; relent and do not bring disaster on your people"…Then the Lord relented and did not bring on his people the disaster he had threatened. Exodus 32: 9-14 (Excerpted)*

Bringing It Home

1. After learning about the importance of candor in a grace-based home, how are you better prepared to respond to your child(ren) if they confess some sort of struggle or sin in their life?

2. What are some ways that you are going to encourage candor in your family?

3. How has this session challenged your perceptions and/or assumptions about parenting?

4. As you commit to being a grace-based parent, what is one thing you are going to do this week to put into practice what you learned in this session?

Bonus Section for Single Parents, Blended Families, and Other Unique Family Configurations

1. Am I doing what I can to remove residue from the past that is distracting me from carrying out the principles of this session? What am I going to do about this?

2. When it comes applying the principles of this session, how am I going to deal with the unique difficulties in my family that are brought on by:

- Fatigue
- Finances
- Guilt
- Anger
- Regret
- Children's suffering

3. Regarding this session, who can I count on to come alongside of me with encouragement and assistance? How am I going to communicate my needs?

Prayer:

Lord, thank you so much that I can reveal my heart to you even when I am angry or struggling with some doubt or sin. Please help me as I respond to my own child(ren) the same way. I want to always speak in an honoring way even if I am correcting or disciplining my child. Please keep the lines of communication open in our home and may our communication always be seasoned with grace. Amen.

Prayer Requests:

_____

_____

_____

We encourage you to read **chapter 10** of Tim's book, ***Grace Based Parenting***, in order to get the most out of the upcoming session of *The Freedom to Make Mistakes*.

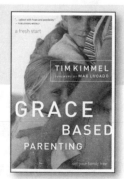

Stay Connected:

Go to www.gracebasedparenting.com for help on how to respond when our children are struggling with some troubling issues or touchy subjects.

GRACE BASED
parenting
VIDEO SERIES
Creating an Atmosphere of Grace

Session 10

The Freedom To Make Mistakes

Aim Them at True Greatness

Build Character
Into Their Hearts

Four Freedoms

Freedom To Be Different	Freedom To Be Vulnerable	Freedom To Be Candid	Freedom To Make Mistakes

Three Inner Needs

Secure Love	Significant Purpose	Strong Hope

Introduction

How parents respond to what happens inside the walls of their home does more to affect the outcome of children's lives than any other single factor.

    A.   A family of origin creates a group identity that ends up defining everyone in that home individually.

    B.   Parents have a huge responsibility to pay attention to the kind of choices their children are making and the assumptions that drive those choices.

    C.   Grace-based parents realize that they walk on feet of clay. This makes them a lot more sensitive to their children when those children disappoint them.

I.   The fourth way parents can create an atmosphere of grace is to give their children the freedom to _____ _____.

    A.   A grace-based atmosphere provides the optimum conditions for dealing with our children's sin.

        •   Grace utilizes a strong connection to their heart rather than fear or _____ to motivate them to righteousness.

        •   Grace doesn't lower standards – if anything, grace is a higher _____.

B. Pleasing God is contingent on a person's faith in Him, not on their ability to maintain a righteous and _____ standard.

> And without faith it is impossible to please God. Hebrews 11:6
>
> ...the righteous will live by faith. Galatians 3:11

C. God wants a _____ to obedience that comes from a love for Him and a trust in Him.

II. **Strident, legalistic, and fear-based families undermine a child's ability to develop a commitment to righteousness that comes from a deep love for God.**

A. These types of homes promote obedience to a _____ rather than obedience to God.

1. In these homes, a child's ability to obey God is dependent on their level of personal will-power rather than a clear understanding of their own weaknesses and a growing love for and trust in God.

> To some who were confident of their own righteousness and looked down on everybody else, Jesus told this parable: "Two men went up to the temple to pray, one a Pharisee and the other a tax collector. The Pharisee stood up and prayed about himself: 'God, I thank you that I am not like other men – robbers, evildoers, adulterers – or even like this tax collector. I fast twice a week and give a tenth of all I get.'
> But the tax collector stood at a distance. He would not even look up to heaven, but beat his breast and said, 'God, have mercy on me, a sinner.'

> *I tell you that this man, rather than the other, went home justified before God. For everyone who exalts himself will be humbled, and he who humbles himself will be exalted."* Luke 18:9-14

2. Guilt and fear can plague children in these homes without the children ever falling into sin.

B. Graceless homes make it very difficult for children to utilize the presence and power of God to gain victory over their bent toward sinful behavior.

III. Grace-based parents don't over-react when their children struggle to do the right thing and make the right choices.

A. In grace-based homes, parents don't preoccupy themselves with trying to keep sin out of their homes.

1. Grace-based homes assume kids will struggle with sin and teaches them to tap God's power to help them get stronger.

2. This attitude helps parents show their kids how to find greater _____ when it comes to their sin.

3. Grace is committed to bringing children up from their sin; legalism puts them on a high standard and works overtime to keep them from falling down.

B. Grace understands that the only real solution for our children's sin is the work of _____ on their behalf.

    1. You can encourage your children to _____ with their sin out in the open where you can talk about it and direct them to the power of Christ.

    2. It is easier for them to have victory when we can help them through their struggles.

> *If you, O LORD, kept a record of sins, O Lord, who could stand? But with you there is forgiveness; therefore you are feared.*
> Psalm 130:3-4

C. Grace avoids condemnation.

> *Therefore, there is now no condemnation for those who are in Christ Jesus, because through Christ Jesus the law of the Spirit of life set me free from the law of sin and death. For what the law was powerless to do in that it was weakened by the sinful nature, God did by sending his own Son in the likeness of sinful man to be a sin offering.* Romans 8:1-3

    1. When children have the freedom to make mistakes, they adopt a humble attitude, experience _____, and express a desire for forgiveness.

Conclusion

Grace-based homes provide the ideal context for kids to process the best and worst of childhood.

A.   Grace-based homes meet a child's true needs for security, significance, and strength, and use each day to meet these needs with love, purpose, and hope.

B.   They are homes where young and restless hearts are free to be different, vulnerable, and candid.

C.   They are homes where children are allowed to struggle with their beliefs and make mistakes on the way to finding their ultimate completion in Jesus Christ.

Remember:

•   Grace is not so much what you do, but how you do it.

•   Grace-based parenting is simply treating your children the way God treats His.

Making This Yours

How did you do on implementing the one practical application you committed to doing this week based on the previous session?

Getting It Started

1. We all make mistakes. Can you give an example of when someone showed you incredible grace? Did it make you want to become a better person or did it give you permission to continue in your mistake?

2. In your own words, explain the difference between license and grace? If we make our standard for righteous behavior "pleasing God," are there some taboos and hang-ups about "Christian" standards that you may have to let go of? Are there some attitudes of the heart that you may have to address?

3. Do you have an example from your past, either involving you or someone else, that illustrates the gracelessness of circumventing consequences? What forms of consequences have you found effective with your own children?

4. Is it your natural inclination to respond or react to your children's disobedience and sin? Put yourself in their shoes; how could responding bring a better outcome?

The Freedom To Make Mistakes

Taking It Deeper

1. Tim reminds us that the only real solution for our child(ren)'s sin is the work of Christ on their behalf. Although it is the parents' responsibility to enforce rules and encourage good behavior, how can we avoid the legalistic trap of only being concerned about their behavior at the expense of their heart?

> *Therefore, there is now no condemnation for those who are in Christ Jesus, because through Christ Jesus the law of the Spirit of life set me free from the law of sin and death. For what the law was powerless to do in that it was weakened by the sinful nature, God did by sending his own Son in the likeness of sinful man to be a sin offering. And so he condemned sin in sinful man, in order that the righteous requirements of the law might be fully met in us, who do not live according to the sinful nature but according to the Spirit.* Romans 8:1-4

2. How has accepting God's grace and becoming a child of God changed your life? Take a moment to write out a prayer for the salvation of your child(ren).

> *How great is the love the Father has lavished on us, that we should be called children of God! And that is what we are!* 1 John 3:1a

Bringing It Home

1. As you look at the model of grace based parenting below, what part have you learned the most about in this DVD study? What section of the house is requiring you to make the most adjustments in your home? What piece would you like prayer for to implement into your own life?

2. Are there some conversations or actions you can take with your child(ren) to show them your own need for Christ's forgiveness and to open up the door for them to dialogue about their struggles with sin?

3. As you commit to being a grace-based parent, what is one thing you are going to do this week to put into practice what you learned in this session?

Bonus Section for Single Parents, Blended Families and Other Unique Family Configurations

1. Am I doing what I can to remove residue from the past that is distracting me from carrying out the principles of this session? What am I going to do about this?

2. When it comes applying the principles of this session, how am I going to deal with the unique difficulties in my family that are brought on by:

- Fatigue
- Finances
- Guilt
- Anger
- Regret
- Children's suffering

3. Regarding this session, who can I count on to come alongside of me with encouragement and assistance? How am I going to communicate my needs?

Prayer:

Lord, thank you so much for this study on grace-based parenting. Thank you that you give us a secure love, a significant purpose, and a strong hope, and thank you that you help us build those into our own children. Help us as we create an atmosphere of grace in our homes by giving our children the freedom to be different, vulnerable, candid, and make mistakes. We need your strength and guidance as we love our children the way you love us – with grace. Amen.

Prayer Requests:

_____

_____

Chapter Eleven of Tim's book, ***Grace Based Parenting***, provides a fitting conclusion to this study. We recommend you read his final remarks titled, "**Evening Grace**".

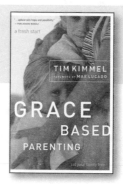

Stay Connected:

This study has provided a great foundation for grace based parenting. To see the rest of the Big Picture of Grace Based Parenting, go to www.gracebasedparenting.com.

We'd love to ask you a few questions about your experience learning to be a grace-based parent. Tell us about you and your story at www.gracebasedparenting.com.

The Big Picture of Grace Based Parenting is built on a foundation of faith in Jesus Christ. If you have never entered into a personal relationship with Christ, there is never a better time than now. Below, you will find all you need to lay that foundation of faith.

GOD LOVES US

For God so loved the world that he gave his one and only Son, that whoever believes in him should not perish but have eternal life. John 3:16

We matter to God. He made us, and He wants to have a relationship with us.

WE ARE SINFUL AND SEPARATED FROM GOD

For all have sinned and fall short of the glory of God. Romans 3:23

But we've rebelled against God. Whether actively or passively, we've all disobeyed Him. And our sins have separated us from Him and broken off the relationship.

THE ULTIMATE CONSEQUENCE OF SIN IS DEATH

For the wages of sin is death… Romans 6:23a

Besides causing separation from God, the sins we have committed must be punished, and the penalty we owe is death. This means physical death as well as spiritual death – eternal separation from God for eternity in a place called hell.

JESUS IS THE ONLY WAY TO GOD

For Christ died for sins once for all…to bring you to God. 1 Peter 3:18

The good news is God loves us so much that He provided a bridge over which we can find forgiveness, restore our relationship, and spend eternity with Him in heaven. He built it by coming to earth as one of us and dying on the cross to pay the death penalty we owed. But it's not enough to know about this, or even agree with it…

WE NEED TO RECEIVE CHRIST PERSONALLY

…to all who received him, to those who believed in his name, he gave the right to become children of God. John 1:12

God has provided this bridge back to Him, but we need to respond to Him by crossing to the other side. We do this by humbly admitting to God that we have rebelled against Him, and we need His forgiveness and leadership. This simple act of trust and obedience results in our being pardoned and our debt being paid. By faith through prayer, you can receive Christ right now. If the following prayer expresses your desire, pray it now.

THE PRAYER OF RESTORATION

Dear Jesus, I know that I need you. Thank you for dying on the cross and paying the price for my sins. I admit that I have fallen short of your standards and ask you to forgive me. Thank you for your forgiveness. Please become the leader of my life and shape me into the person you want me to be. Amen

The Bible says that the angels rejoice when someone accepts Christ as their Savior (Luke 15:10). Make sure you tell someone your good news!

For more information or to order online go to Shop.FamilyMatters.net.

Books

Grace Based Parenting
This book is a must for parents who want to love their kids the way God loves his. With humor and pathos, it goes into depth on how to meet our children's inner heart needs and grant the four freedoms that can make an atmosphere of grace a permanent condition in your home.

Raising Kids Who Turn Out Right
With warmth and conviction, Dr. Tim Kimmel outlines a plan for building your child from the inside out by transferring character – faith, integrity, poise, disciplines, endurance and courage- into their heart.

Raising Kids for True Greatness

Wouldn't it be great to have kids who are humble, grateful, generous and have a servant's heart? Dr. Tim Kimmel shows you how to turn greatness into the DNA of your own life so you can pass it on to your children. This book also helps you prepare your child to answer the three biggest questions of life and is filled with many "Top Ten" lists for applying the principles of true greatness in everyday life.

Little House on the Freeway
Don't let busyness and the temptation to "keep up with the Joneses" keep you from the peace and incredible quality of relationships God created for you. This book will empower you and your family with confidence and practical, stress-saving skills as you take the off-ramp to sanity, peace and family harmony.

Why Christian Kids Rebel
This book provides help and hope for parents dealing with a rebellious teen and teaches them how to lead that child back into a walk of faith. This book also offers a doable plan for parents of young children who want to avoid having them walk away from God in a few short years.

Grace Filled Marriage

Grace-Filled Marriage explores the daily reality of a life lived out with a commitment to treating our spouse the way God treats us—with grace. In this provocative look at love, we'll see how God's grace plays out in our marriage as we navigate through the areas of sex, kids, conflict, aging, and endings . . . gracefully.

Homegrown Heroes

Of all the values and skills we need to build into our children's hearts, courage tops the list. Courage is what will motivate our children to do what they ought to do in any given situation. This sweetly powerful book will turn your good intentions into a plan that works to give your children their best shot at a great and meaningful life.

High Cost of High Control

No one likes to be controlled, including our kids. Life can be a whole lot more pleasant around your house when you determine to keep your kids under control, rather than try to control them. Dr. Tim Kimmel gives you the biblical strategy for breaking free from the pain of controlling people and how to avoid being a high-controller yourself.

Connecting Church and Home

We are faced with a culture of busy churches and overwhelmed families that need a clear plan to pass a spiritual legacy to the hearts of their kids. Dr. Tim Kimmel shows how churches and parents can work together in a grace-based partnership to make each other's efforts more impactful.

Extreme Grandparenting: The Ride of Your Life

Are you ready to take grandparenting to the next level? You'll learn how to make the most of this significant opportunity to imprint the next generation with grace. Discover how you can be not only a mentor but a spiritual rock for your grandchildren. It is full of fresh new ideas to connect to the heart of your grandchildren.

In Praise of Plan B

Life doesn't always go according to plan – your plan that is. These twenty light hearted, encouraging stories will remind you that making the most of whatever happens is a much better way to go through life. You'll laugh until you cry and cry until you need to laugh as you look at life as it can be when you step aside and let God call the shots.

Tools

Kids Flag Page

Consider this the operating manual that should have come with each of your kids – but didn't. This colorful and engaging game is a fun way for parents to interact with their kids and truly discover the heart of each child – who God created them to be. It also comes with an eye opening book that thoroughly outlines a strategy for each of your children, including those strong-willed ones in your home.

Video Studies

The Grace Based Parenting Video Series

Part 1: Creating an Atmosphere of Grace

This is a fun, refreshing small group study that gives parents a realistic job description for raising spiritually strong children who grow up with a sense of calm and a heart full of purpose. As you watch the DVD and use the helpful discussion guide, you will learn to meet your children's inner heart needs and grant the four freedoms that can make an atmosphere of grace a permanent condition in your home.

Part 2: Building Character

This exciting study is a practical strategy for raising kids who turn out right by instilling character into their hearts. These seven powerful sessions, with helpful discussion guides and leaders' tools, will show you how to model and teach your children about faith, integrity, poise, disciplines, endurance and courage.

Part 3: Aiming at True Greatness

This eye-opening study exposes our culture's definition of success (wealth, beauty, power and fame) as a goal unworthy of our pursuit. Instead, it describes the spiritual adventure we can live when we aim our children at a higher goal – True Greatness. The DVD and discussion guide present four characteristics of truly great people along with many other helpful insights designed to equip your children to answer life's three biggest questions.

The Hurried Family Video Study

In this age of stress and crazy schedules, you can never have enough help and hope amidst the hurry. This small group study will empower you and your family with confidence and practical, stress-saving skills as you take the off-ramp to sanity, peace and family harmony. Includes powerful discussion guide and leaders' tools.

Extreme Grandparenting: The Ride of Your Life

As a grandparent, you have a valuable opportunity to influence and connect to the heart of your grandchildren. Make the most of it by gathering a group of like-minded grandparents and going through this interactive study together. You'll receive practical teaching and enjoy lively discussions as you learn how to play a key role in the generation that you will one day leave in charge.

Basic Training for a Few Good Men

This push and play study couldn't be easier for men's groups and retreats. Complete with discussion guides and leaders' tools, this exciting study gives husbands and dads marching orders for moral and spiritual leadership in the key areas of family, work, community and church – all delivered powerfully, with warmth and humor.

Where To Go From Here: *A Guide for Going Deeper*

Now that you have finished this foundational study on grace based parenting, it's important to ask yourself, "Where do I go from here?" Our follow-up resources complete the "big picture" and equip you to let grace based parenting transform your family and your own life as well.

Encouragement and reinforcement are key ingredients to any new endeavor. Talking and praying through these concepts with each other or other parents will help you develop the mindset of a truly great parent.

We encourage you to:

Do another Video Study

We have many more exciting video studies for you and your group. A complete list can be found on the resources pages of this workbook or at our website, familymatters.net.

Read a book

Each book that Family Matters offers has its own small group study guide in the back which equips parents to make these principles a lifestyle, helps them remember what they just learned and provides real life examples of how to apply these ideas to daily life.

Lead a study

Why not take it a step further and start your own group? Maybe you could do this in your neighborhood, school or church. One of the best ways to learn something well is to teach it to others. We have fantastic facilitator support material on our website for all those who step out to lead one of these transformational studies.

Attend a Conference

For an exciting and equipping experience, come to one of our fun, fast paced events. Go to familymatters.net to see where we are holding one of our next life-changing Raising Truly Great Kids Conferences.

Where To Go From Here: *A Guide for Going Deeper*

Host a Conference

Bring the **Raising Truly Great Kids Conference** to your church and community. Let us tell you about the incredible possibilities available for hearing the grace based message. For more information, go to www.raisingtrulygreatkids.com.

Stay Connected

Our web community is there for you as you raise your family and build grace based relationships. Go to familymatters.net and take advantage of all of our helpful family tools.

- www.familymatters.net (a treasure trove of help and hope for your family)
- Heart of the Home (a free quarterly e-magazine)
- Bible in a Year daily email
- Dinner Dialogue (conversation starters with your kids)
- Famlly Matters Minute (grace based nuggets of wisdom for your parenting journey)
- Family Matters' Blog, Facebook, and Twitter

About Family Matters

> ### The vision of Family Matters
> is to see families transformed by God's grace into instruments of reformation and restoration.

Family Matters educates, encourages and equips families to:
- live relevant, joyful and victorious lives
- bring the best out of each other in their daily relationships
- pass a legacy of God's grace from one generation to the next

Family Matters offers families help and hope for every age and stage of life through our:
- Conferences and Keynote events
- Best selling books
- Practical, well-researched Video studies
- Interactive and transformational family tools

You Can Be a Part of Building Strong Families

Family Matters is a non-profit, charitable organization committed to strengthening the vital relationships within families. It is a member of the Evangelical Council for Financial Accountability.

The faithful donations of people who share a kindred heart for strong Christian homes enables Family Matters to create new ways and means to bring health and strength to today's families.

If you would like to get more information on how to make Family Matters part of your charitable giving portfolio, please call 1.800.467.4596 or go online to www.familymatters.net.

Building Grace Based Relationships is what Family Matters is all about.

Fill-in-the-Blank Answer Guide

Session 1:
great kids
impact
grace
difference
how
mirrors
influence
society

Session 2:
competes
mislead
handicap
resist
moral
obedience
controlled
spiritual
sub-culture
flawed
alternative
accident

Session 3:
balance
toxic
arbitrary
insults
cheapens
truth
balance

Session 4:
Love
Purpose
Hope
action
incomplete
compete
earn
definition
accept
affiliated
affection

Session 5:
difference
potential
General
Specific
Relational
Spiritual
affirmation
attention
admonition

Session 6:
transfer
helpless
abilities
adventure
safe
strong
accomplishments

Session 7:
atmosphere
magnify
different
sinful
symbols
internal
biblical
Bible
heart
struggle
potential

Session 8:
tender mercy
vulnerable
masks
attacked
connection
common sense

Session 9:
candid
honor
beliefs
remain calm
others-oriented
encourage

Session 10:
make mistakes
guilt
holiness
moral
commitment
standard
victory
Christ
struggle
remorse